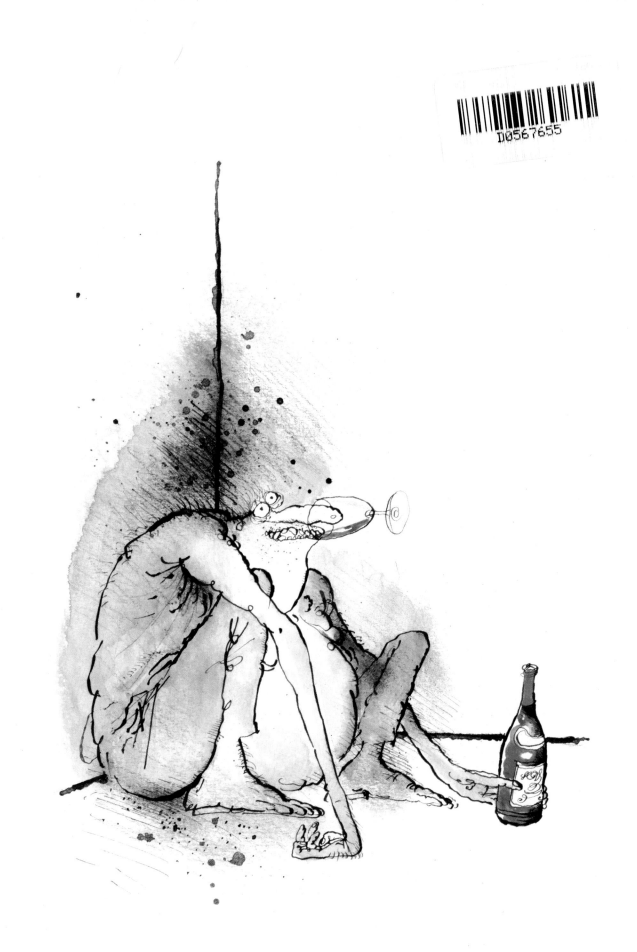

Wine Ceremonies of the World
TRANSYLVANIA
Legendary rites hailing the apparition of Noble Rot

Something in the Cellar...

RONALD SEARLE'S

Wonderful World of Wine

TEN SPEED PRESS

1๑

Ten Speed Press
P.O. Box 7123
Berkeley, California 94707

This collection first published in 1986 by Souvenir Press Ltd.,
43 Great Russell Street, London WC1B 3PA
and simultaneously in Canada

Some of the drawings in this album
first appeared in
The Subtle Alchemist by George Rainbird
& Ronald Searle, Michael Joseph: London 1973;
Pariscope magazine, Paris 1973;
Paris! Paris! by Irwin Shaw & Ronald Searle,
Harcourt Brace Jovanovitch: New York 1977
&
Ronald Searle's Illustrated Winespeak,
Souvenir Press: London 1983.

The majority of the colour pages, now in
the Cooper-Hewitt Museum, New York City
and in the private collection of
Mr. & Mrs. John Goelet, New York,
were originally conceived to promote
the vineyards of John Goelet:
CLOS DU VAL
in the Napa Valley, California
&
TALTARNI VINEYARDS
Moonambel, Australia.

The rest of the drawings
are new and appear for the
first time in this collection.

ISBN 0-89815-235-6

Printed in Korea

The Wonderful World of Wine
CONNOISSEURS

GREAT WINE CEREMONIES
Annual Reunion of the Confrérie of Cork Sniffers

WINE CEREMONIES OF THE WORLD
The Annual Non-Arrival of the English Grape Ceremony

How to open a bottle of wine

HIGH PRIEST

Wine Ceremonies of the World
FRANCE
Annual Festival of Welcome to Italian Wines

HARMONY

Wine Ceremonies of the World
GERMANY
The Ancient, Noble (and Secret) Ceremony of Slashing the Trockenbeerenauslese

The Wonderful World of Wine
THE JAPANESE WINE CEREMONY

The Wonderful World of Wine
SWITZERLAND
Bottling time

Wine Ceremonies of the World
ITALY
Inauguration of the First Authentic (and Indisputable)
Denominazione di Origine Controllata e Garantita

THE NOBLE GRAPE

Ah, my Beloved, fill the cup...

Wine Ceremonies of the World
MEXICO
Everyday Ceremony of Trying to Stand Up to Mañana

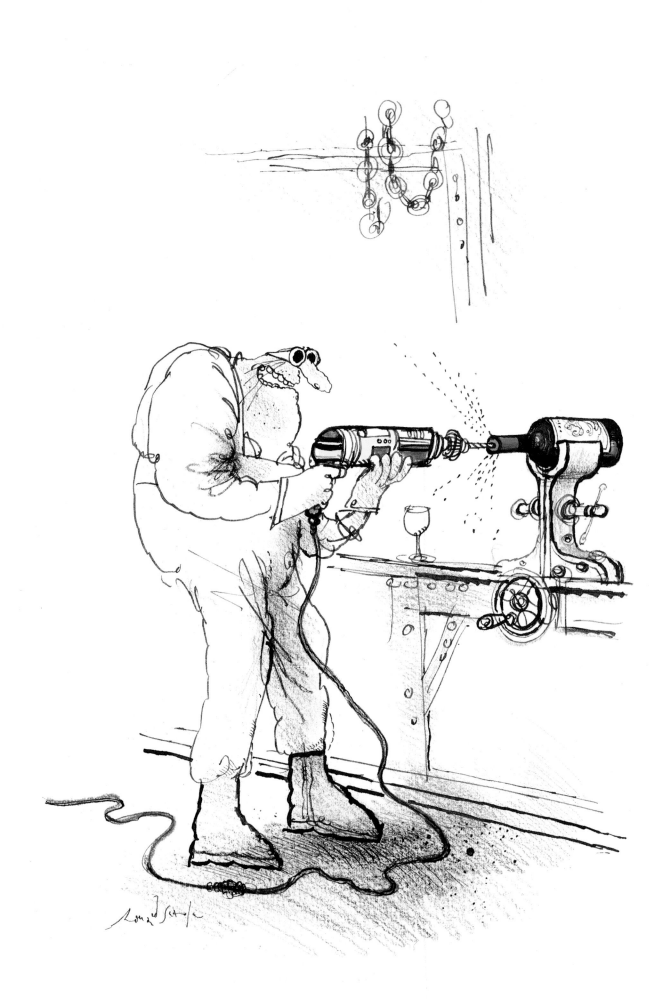

Wine Ceremonies of the World
SPAIN
Ancient Festival of Hoofing the Rioja

BACCHANALIA INVESTMENTWISE

Wine Ceremonies of the World
U.S.S.R.
Annual Ceremony of Accepting Kremlin Rouge

IMPATIENCE

The Wonderful World of Wine
A CHEERFUL BUNCH

Wine Ceremonies of the World
IRELAND
Touching and rather dampish Ceremony of Wailing O'er the Wine

Wine Ceremonies of the World
U.S.A.
Blessing the Grapes, Californian Style

The Wonderful World of Wine
OLYMPUS
Nectar Time

The Wonderful World of Wine
PORTUGAL
Any Old Port in a Storm

Great Wine Ceremonies
CYPRUS
Doing the Splits

Wine Ceremonies of the World
SCOTLAND
The Squeezing of the Bonnie Malted Grape

Wine Ceremonies of the World
SOUTH AFRICA

Colourful Ceremony of Offering Limited Recognition to the Black Grape

Wine Ceremonies of the World
HOLLAND
Historical but somewhat yucky ceremony of Pulling Out the Finger

Wine Ceremonies of the World
BYZANTIUM
Frustrating Ceremony of Trying to Round-up Square Grapes

How to open a bottle of wine

The Wonderful World of Wine
VINOLYMPICS

Wine Ceremonies of the World
THE EUROPEAN COMMUNITY

Non-stop Festival of Sour Grapes

A jug of wine, a loaf of bread and Thou . . .

The Wonderful World of Wine
IRAN
Latter-day miracle. Turning Wine into Water

Wine Ceremonies of the World
BRAZIL

Traditional Ceremony of Facing up to Room Temperature

The Wonderful World of Wine
CHINA
Inventor of People's Pinot surviving yet another felicitation

Wine Ceremonies of the World
AUSTRALIA
Uncorking the Kangarouge

The Wonderful World of Wine
GREECE
Keeping an Eye on the Press

Wine Ceremonies of the World
EGYPT
Arrival of the Ptolemy Nouveau

The Wonderful World of Wine
U.S.A.
Striking it Rich in Texas

The Wonderful World of Wine
EL SALVADOR
Pause for a drop of rouge du pays